BEHIND THE SCENES BIOGRAPHIES

WHAT YOU NEVER KNEW ABOUT POST MALONE

by Mari Bolte

CAPSTONE PRESS
a capstone imprint

This is an unauthorized biography.

Published by Spark, an imprint of Capstone
1710 Roe Crest Drive, North Mankato, Minnesota 56003
capstonepub.com

Library of Congress Cataloging-in-Publication Data
Names: Bolte, Mari, author.
Title: What you never knew about Post Malone / Mari Bolte.
Description: North Mankato : Capstone Press, 2026. | Series: Behind the scenes biographies | Includes bibliographical references and index. | Audience: Ages 9-11 | Audience: Grades 4-6 | Summary: "Post Malone was the first-ever artist to have a number-one album on Billboard's Top Country, Rap, and Rock & Alternative charts. But do you know what his real name is? What about the name of his high school band? High-interest details and bold photos of Post's high-profile life will enthrall reluctant and striving readers, while carefully leveled text will leave them feeling confident"— Provided by publisher.
Identifiers: LCCN 2025012049 (print) | LCCN 2025012050 (ebook) | ISBN 9798875253393 (hardcover) | ISBN 9798875253348 (paperback) | ISBN 9798875253355 (pdf) | ISBN 9798875253362 (epub) | ISBN 9798875253379 (kindle edition)
Subjects: LCSH: Malone, Post, 1995-—Juvenile literature. | Rap musicians—United States—Biography—Juvenile literature. | Singers—United States—Biography—Juvenile literature. | LCGFT: Biographies.
Classification: LCC ML3930.M295 B65 2026 (print) | LCC ML3930.M295 (ebook) | DDC 782.421649092 [B]—dc23/eng/20250325
LC record available at https://lccn.loc.gov/2025012049
LC ebook record available at https://lccn.loc.gov/2025012050

Editorial Credits
Editor: Mandy Robbins; Designer: Elijah Blue; Media Researcher: Rebekah Hubstenberger; Production Specialist: Tori Abraham

Quote Source
p. 21 "You're entitled . . ." Weinstein, Max. "Starlito and Post Malone Speak on Going at Each Other on Twitter." *XXLmag.com*, xxlmag.com/starlito-post-malone-beef-interview-twitter/?utm_source=tsmclip&utm_medium=referral, Accessed 4/1/2025.

Image Credits
Alamy: TCD/Prod.DB, 19; Associated Press: Perry Knotts, cover; Getty Images: Daniel Boczarski/Redferns, 11, Amy Sussman, 4, 21 (middle), Brett Carlsen, 17, Greg Doherty, 20 (middle left), Jamie Squire, 9, John Shearer, 15, Kevin Mazur, 28, Kevin Winter, 20 (bottom right), Matt Winkelmeyer, 23, Michael Ochs Archives, 16, Paras Griffin, 20 (middle right), Phil Walter, 13, Randy Shropshire, 12, Rebecca Sapp, 20 (bottom left), Robert Kamau, 27 (right), Scott Dudelson, 25, Terry Wyatt, 26; Shutterstock: Alexander_P, 10, Artoholics, 24 (flames), Ben Houdijk, 7, Bespana, 21 (hearts), Bilbo Baggins, 18, Gun2becontinued, 8, Humdan, 24 (stylized letters), Illerlok_xolms (line designs), cover and throughout, Kathy Hutchins, 14, SkyroseStudio, 22, Telkraf.id, 27 (middle), thanya, 29

Printed and bound in China. 006459

TABLE OF CONTENTS

Words in **bold** are in the glossary.

RECORDING GREATNESS

Post Malone has sold more than 80 million records. He's a master of many music styles. Post can sing country and pop. He can rap and even act! People instantly recognize his fashion and his tattoos.

What don't you know about this singer-songwriter? Time to find out!

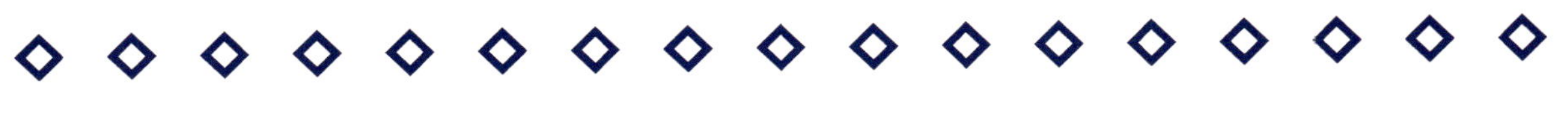

TRUE OR **FALSE?**

You know everything about Post Malone.

True or false?

1. **Post's real name is Postal B. Malone.**
2. **Post started recording his own music when he was 16.**
3. **Post was born on New Year's Eve.**
4. **Post has performed at the Super Bowl.**
5. **Post had a song on the soundtrack for *Spider-Man: Into the Spider-Verse.***
6. **Post's dad was a music producer.**
7. ***Hunt: Showdown* is Post's favorite video game.**

FACT

Post Malone is a made-up name. An online rap name generator came up with it.

1. FALSE (It's Austin Richard Post.) **2.** TRUE **3.** FALSE (He was born on the 4th of July.) **4.** TRUE **5.** TRUE

6. FALSE (He was a DJ, among other things.) **7.** TRUE

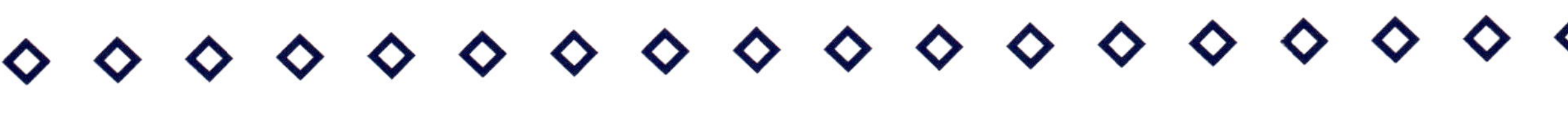

HEROIC TALENT

Post loves playing *Guitar Hero*. He started when he was 12 years old. Post got so good that he decided to try the real thing. His mom got him a guitar for Christmas. He learned from YouTube videos.

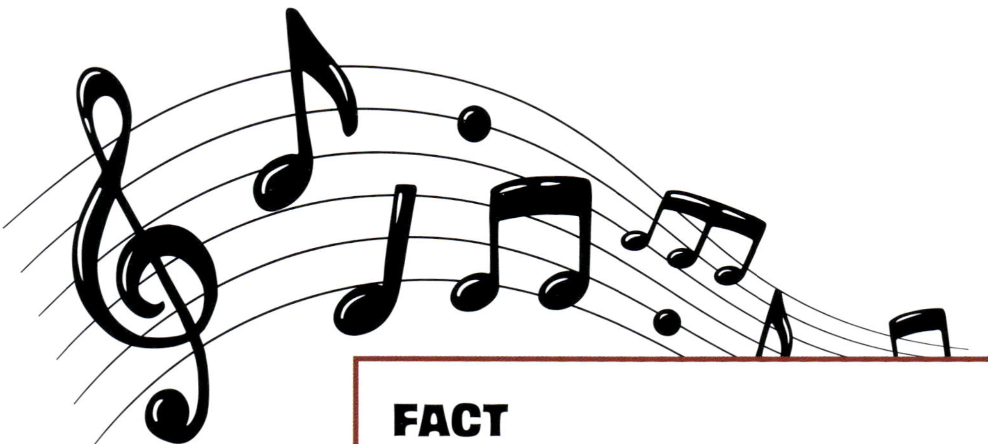

FACT

In 2024, Post worked with a mobile gaming company called Backbone. They made a **limited-edition** video game controller. It was see-through, green, and glowed in the dark.

In high school, Post joined a band. Ashley's Arrival played hardcore metal. He had tried out for another band called Crown the Empire. At the **audition**, a string on his guitar broke. He didn't make the cut.

Crown the Empire

ATTENTION:
STAR ON BOARD

In February 2015, Post released "White Iverson." It had 1 million listens in its first month. His **debut** album, *Stoney*, came out December of 2016. It spent 77 weeks on Billboard's Top 10 R&B/Hip-Hop Albums list. It broke Michael Jackson's record of 34 years.

Michael Jackson

Post is known for his goofy, friendly personality. Justin Bieber is one of Post's good friends. Taylor Swift is another. Both have worked with Post to make new music.

"All My Friends" was a **collaboration** with 21 Savage. The song talks about how fame has changed his friendships.

21 Savage and Post Malone

Taylor Swift and Post Malone

In 2023, Post broke the Beatles' record of 54 years. He had nine songs in the top 20 spots on Billboard's Hot 100. He was also the first artist in history to have a number one album on Billboard's Top Country, Rap, and Rock & Alternative charts.

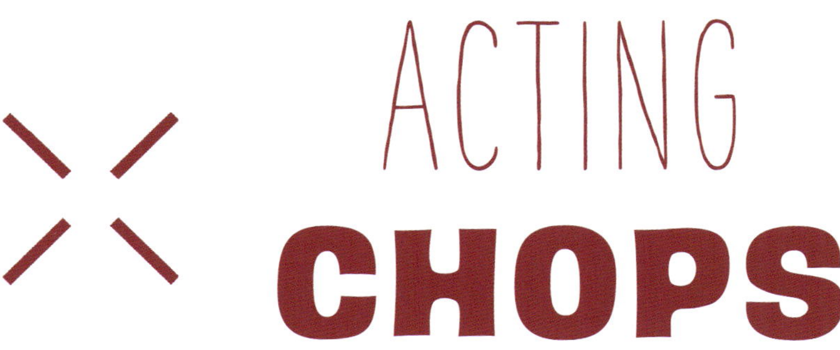

ACTING CHOPS

Why stop with music? Post is an actor too! His first movie was *Spenser Confidential*. He didn't even audition. Actor Mark Wahlberg wanted him in the movie. Post was so good that they turned two roles into one. That way he had a bigger part.

Post played an inmate in *Spenser Confidential*.

Not everyone is a Post Malone fan. Some celebs have made **diss tracks** about him. They start fights on X. Post doesn't let negativity keep him down.

Post Haters:

Lil B

Charlamagne tha God

Yelawolf

Earl Sweatshirt

"You're entitled to an opinion and I don't care if you don't like me."

–Post Malone

"POSTMATES" MALONE

Post loves chicken nuggets, biscuits, and garlic knots. He says he eats like a four-year-old. In 2018, Postmates named him their most dedicated customer. He had spent over $40,000 on the delivery app. That's 660 orders across 52 cities!

FACT

In 2025, Oreo released Post Malone Oreos. They have one chocolate cookie, one golden cookie, and a salted-caramel crème center.

UNIQUE LOOK

Post has more than 70 tattoos. In 2018, he got "Always" under his right eye. It says "Tired" under his left. Other tattoos are for his daughter. He has kept her name a secret. But her initials, DDP, are tattooed on his forehead.

GIVING BACK

Post felt cooped up during the COVID-19 **pandemic**. He knew others felt the same way. In 2020, he raised $500,000 with a Nirvana **tribute** concert. It streamed on YouTube. The proceeds went to COVID-19 relief.

FACT

Post's lifestyle brand, Shaboink, donated 40,000 face masks and 10,000 pairs of Crocs to healthcare workers during the pandemic.

Happy 15th BIRTHDAY!
YOU SAVED ME

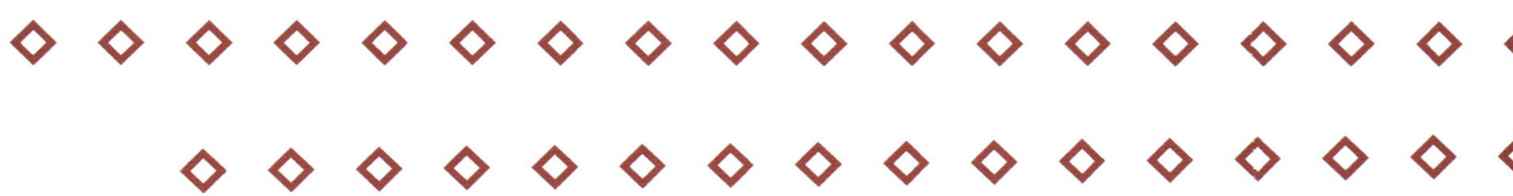

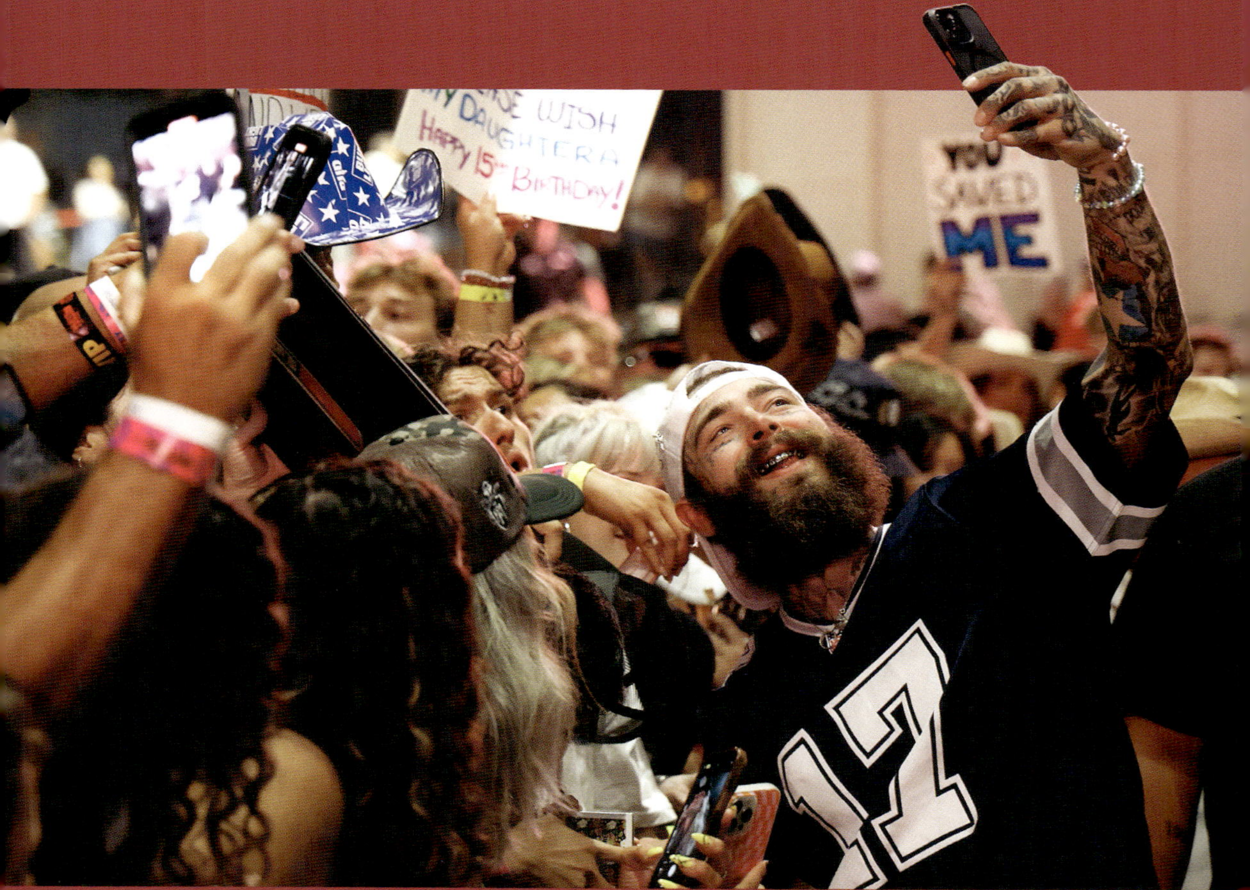

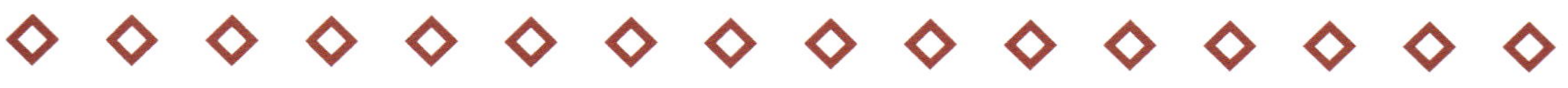

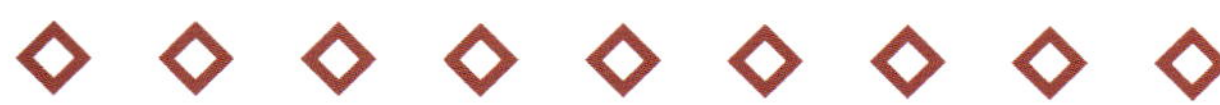

Post likes to give back. In 2022, gamers watched Post livestream on Twitch. He raised $200,000 for four different **charities**. The next year, he donated a signed guitar to the Utah Honor Flight Program. This program helps **veterans** travel to Washington, D.C. to see war memorials.

FACT
In 2024, Post left a waitress a $20,000 tip on Christmas Eve.

Glossary

audition (aw-DISH-uhn)—a tryout performance

charity (CHAYR-uh-tee)—a group that raises money or collects goods to help people in need

collaboration (kuh-lab-uh-RAY-shuhn)—two or more people working together

debut (day-BYOO)—a first showing

diss track (DISS TRAK)—a song written to mock or disrespect another person or group

limited-edition (LIM-uh-tuhd uh-DISH-uhn)—a version of an item with only a small amount available for purchase

pandemic (pan-DEM-ik)—a disease that spreads over the entire world and affects many people

tribute (TRIH-byoot)—a performance that shows respect and admiration for someone or something

veteran (VET-uh-ruhn)—a person who served in the armed forces

Read More

Lawson, Carlie. *Post Malone*. Broomall, PA: Mason Crest, 2020.

Lüsted, Marcia Amidon. *Post Malone: Rapper, Singer, and Songwriter*. Minneapolis: Abdo Publishing, 2020.

Marx, Mandy R. *What You Never Knew about Taylor Swift*. North Mankato, MN: Capstone Press, 2022.

Internet Sites

Billboard: Post Malone
billboard.com/artist/post-malone/

Biography: Post Malone
biography.com/musicians/a62407330/post-malone

Fun Facts About Post Malone–Did You Know?
lovinlifemusicfest.com/news/fun-facts-about-post-malone-did-you-know/

Index

About the Author

Mari Bolte is the author and editor of hundreds of children's books Every book is her favorite book as long as readers learned something and enjoyed themselves!